First American edition 2013.
First UK edition 2012.

Tharpa Publications US Office
47 Sweeney Road
Glen Spey, NY
12737, USA

Tharpa Publications UK Office
Conishead Priory
Ulverston, Cumbria
LA12 9QQ, UK

Tharpa Publications is part of the
New Kadampa Tradition – International Kadampa Buddhist Union (NKT-IKBU).
Tharpa has offices around the world and Tharpa books are published in most major languages.

Text and Illustrations
© New Kadampa Tradition – International Kadampa Buddhist Union 2012, 2013

Library of Congress Control Number: 2012955586

ISBN: 978-1-61606-023-7 – paperback

Set in Candara by Tharpa Publications.

Paper supplied from well-managed forests and other controlled
sources, and certified in accordance with the rules of the
Forest Stewardship Council.

WHAT IS BUDDHISM?

GESHE KELSANG GYATSO

Buddhism for Children Level Three

THARPA PUBLICATIONS
US • UK • CANADA
AUSTRALIA • ASIA

What is Buddhism?

Tathagata, Foe Destroyer, Completely Perfect Buddha,

Glorious Conqueror Shakyamuni

Buddhism is the practice of Buddha's teachings, also called "Dharma," which means "protection." By practicing Buddha's teachings, living beings are permanently protected from suffering. The founder of Buddhism is Buddha Shakyamuni, who showed how to accomplish the ultimate goal of living beings, the attainment of enlightenment, at Bodh Gaya in India in 589 BC. At the request of the gods Indra and Brahma, Buddha then began to give his profound teachings, or "turned the Wheel of Dharma." Buddha gave 84,000 teachings, and from these precious teachings Buddhism developed in this world.

We should know that although we want to be happy all the time we do not know how to do this, and we are always destroying our own happiness by developing anger, negative views, and negative intentions. We are always trying to escape from problems, even in our dreams, but we do not know how to free ourself from suffering and problems. Because we do not understand the real nature of things, we are always creating our own suffering and problems

Tathagata Complete Subduer with the Essence of Vajra

Tathagata Jewel of Radiant Light • *Tathagata Powerful King of the Nagas*

by performing inappropriate or non-virtuous actions. We need to practice Buddha's teachings because there is no other real method to solve human problems. For example, because modern technology often causes more suffering and dangers, it cannot be a real method to solve human problems.

The source of all our daily problems and suffering is our uncontrolled desire, also known as "attachment." Since beginningless time, because we have had uncontrolled desire for the fulfillment of our own wishes, we have performed various kinds of non-virtuous actions—actions that harm others. As a result, we continually experience various kinds of suffering and miserable conditions in life after life without end. When our wishes are not fulfilled we usually experience unpleasant feelings, such as unhappiness or depression; this is our own problem because we are so attached to the fulfillment of our wishes. When we lose a close friend we experience pain and unhappiness, but this is only because we have no ability to control our desire. When we lose our possessions and the things that we like, we experience unhappiness and we

Tathagata Leader of the Heroes

Tathagata Glorious Pleasure • *Tathagata Jewel Fire*

become upset and angry. This is because we have uncontrolled desire for these things. If we were able to control our desire there would be no basis to experience these problems. Many people are engaged in fighting, criminal actions, and even warfare; all these actions arise from their uncontrolled desire for the fulfillment of their own wishes. In this way, we can see that there is not a single problem experienced by living beings that does not come from their uncontrolled desire. This proves that unless we control our desire, our problems will never cease. Therefore, anyone—whether Buddhist or non-Buddhist—who does not wish to experience problems and suffering should learn to control their desire through training in the particular meditations that are presented in Buddha's teachings.

We should understand that our problems do not exist outside of ourself, but are part of our mind that experiences unpleasant feelings. When our computer, for example, has a problem we usually say, "I have a problem," but in reality it is the computer's problem and not our problem. The

Tathagata Jewel Moonlight

Tathagata Meaningful to Behold • *Tathagata Jewel Moon*

computer's problem is an outer problem, and our problem, which is our own unpleasant feeling, is an inner problem. These two problems are completely different. We need to solve the computer's problem by repairing it, and we need to solve our own problem by controlling our desire for the computer. Even if we keep solving the computer's problems, if we are unable to control our desire for the computer we will continually experience new problems related to the computer. It is the same with our house, our money, our friendships, and so forth. Because of mistakenly believing that outer problems are their own problems, most people seek ultimate refuge in the wrong objects. As a result, their suffering and problems never end.

For as long as we are unable to control our delusions such as our uncontrolled desire, we will have to experience suffering and problems continually, throughout this life and in life after life without end. Because we are bound tightly by the rope of uncontrolled desire to the enjoyments of samsara, the cycle of impure life, it is impossible for us to be free from suffering and

Tathagata Stainless One

Tathagata Bestower of Glory • *Tathagata Pure One*

problems unless we practice Buddha's teachings, Dharma. Understanding this, we should develop and maintain the strong wish to abandon the root of suffering—uncontrolled desire. This wish is called "renunciation," and arises from our wisdom.

Buddha's teachings are scientific methods to solve the problems of all living beings permanently. By putting his teachings into practice we will be able to control our desire and because of this we will be permanently free from all our suffering and problems. From this alone we can understand how precious and important his teachings, the Dharma, are for everyone. As mentioned above, all our problems come from uncontrolled desire, and because there is no method to control our desire other than Dharma it is clear that only Dharma is the actual method to solve our daily problems.

We know that everybody says, "My mind, my mind," but if someone were to ask us, "What is the mind?" we would have no clear answer. Some

Tathagata Transforming with Purity

Tathagata Water Deity • *Tathagata God of Water Deities*

people say that our brain is the mind, but this is incorrect. The brain cannot be the mind because it is simply a part of the body; we can see it directly with our eyes and it can even be photographed. On the other hand, the mind is not a part of the body; we cannot see it with our eyes and it cannot be photographed. Therefore it is clear that the brain is not the mind. We can find a clear answer to the question, "What is the mind?" from Buddha's teachings.

Buddha gave clear and detailed explanations about the mind as follows. The mind is something whose nature is empty like space, which has never possessed form, shape, or color, and whose function is to perceive and understand objects. There are three different levels of mind: gross, subtle and very subtle mind. During our dreams, we have dream awareness through which the various kinds of dream things appear to us. This awareness is a subtle mind because it is difficult to recognize. During deep sleep we have only one mental awareness, which perceives emptiness alone.

Tathagata Glorious Excellence

Tathagata Glorious Sandalwood • Tathagata Endless Splendour

This awareness is called the "clear light of sleep," and it is the very subtle mind because it is extremely difficult to recognize.

During the waking day we have waking awareness through which various kinds of waking things appear to us. This awareness is a gross mind because it is not difficult to recognize. When we fall asleep our gross mind, or waking awareness, dissolves into our subtle mind of sleep. At the same time, all our appearances of the waking world become non-existent; and when we experience deep sleep, our subtle mind of sleep dissolves into our very subtle mind of sleep, the clear light of sleep. At this stage, we have become like a person who has died. Then, because of our maintaining a karmic connection with this life, from our clear light of sleep, our gross mind, or waking awareness, will arise again and various kinds of waking things appear to us again.

The process of sleeping is very similar to the process of dying. The difference between these two is that when we are dying our gross and subtle minds will dissolve into our very subtle mind of death, known as the "clear light of death." Then, because of our karmic connection with this life ceasing, our very subtle mind leaves this body, goes to the next life and enters a new body, and then all the various kinds of things of the next life will appear to us. Everything will be completely new.

From this explanation about the mind we can understand clearly the existence of our future lives, so that we can prepare now for the happiness and freedom of our countless future lives through practicing Buddha's teachings, Dharma. There is no greater meaning than this. Our present life is only one single life but our future lives are countless. Therefore, there is no doubt that future lives are more important than this life.

The teachings of Buddha presented in this book are principally for children, but anyone who studies and practices these teachings will experience great results.

About the Author

Geshe Kelsang Gyatso, or Geshe-la as he is affectionately known by his students, is a world-renowned Buddhist meditation master who has pioneered the introduction of modern Buddhism into contemporary society.

Through his personal example and his public teachings and writings he demonstrates how everyone, whether Buddhist or non-Buddhist, can learn to become wiser and more compassionate by following the advice of Buddha.

Geshe Kelsang is the founder of the International Kadampa Schools Project, which was inaugurated in September 2012 with the opening of the first International Kadampa Primary School in Derbyshire, England.

The Eight Auspicious Symbols

Symbolizing the spiritual path to enlightenment

Precious Umbrella
Come under the great umbrella of Buddhism

Precious Fish

Maintain harmony and joy all the time

Precious Vase

Take the precious jewels of wisdom and compassion
from the treasure vase of Kadam Dharma

Precious Lotus

Enjoy the purity of your mind and actions

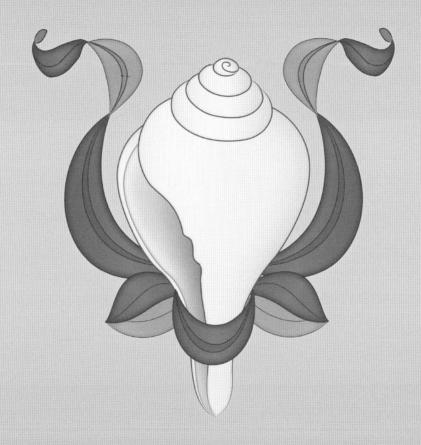

Precious Conch

Listen to the precious sound of the conch of Dharma
and contemplate and meditate on its meaning

Precious Indestructible Knot

Apply great effort to attain enlightenment

Precious Victory Banner

Be victorious over the enemy of your delusions

Precious Wheel of Dharma

Benefit others by turning the Wheel of Dharma

The *Buddhism for Children* series:

The **Buddhism for Children** series invites children to make a journey of self-discovery and self-improvement to help them realize their full potential.

The purpose is not to convert them to Buddhism but simply to show how everyone, Buddhist or non-Buddhist, can learn something from the teachings of Buddha.

These books address the reader in a mature fashion, using the life and teachings of Buddha as a basis for exploring many of the issues and concerns that confront children today.

Although these books are written principally for children, anyone who wants a clear explanation of the essence of Buddhism and how it applies to modern living will benefit greatly from reading them.

For more books, audio, and artwork on Buddhism and Meditation visit: **www.tharpa.com**

Buddhism for Children Level 1
The Story of Angulimala

Buddhism for Children Level 2
The Story of Buddha

Buddhism for Children Level 3
What is Buddhism?

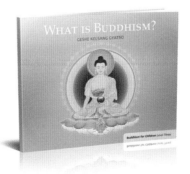

Buddhism for Children Level 4
What is Meditation?

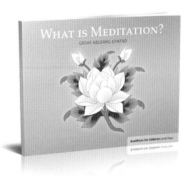